Between
TIME
and
TIMBUKTU

BOOKS BY

Kurt Vonnegut, Jr.

Between TIME and TIMBUKTU

or
Prometheus-5

A SPACE FANTASY
BASED ON MATERIALS BY

Kurt Vonnegut, Jr.

DESIGNED BY JOEL SCHICK

WITH PHOTOGRAPHS BY

JILL KREMENTZ

AND FROM THE

NET PLAYHOUSE

PRODUCTION

DELTA

A DELTA BOOK
Published by
DELL PUBLISHING CO., INC.
1 Dag Hammarskjold Plaza
New York, N.Y. 10017

Delta ® TM 755118, Dell Publishing Co., Inc.
This edition printed by arrangement with
Delacorte Press/Seymour Lawrence
New York, New York 10017
Printed in the United States of America
Fourth Printing
Library of Congress Cataloging in Publication Data

Cast

(IN ORDER OF APPEARANCE)

Stony Stevenson
WILLIAM HICKEY

Contest Announcer
BRUCE MORROW

Mrs. Stevenson
DORTHA DUCKWORTH

Walter Gesundheit
RAY GOULDING

Bud Williams, Jr.
BOB ELLIOTT

Col. Donald "Tex" Pirandello
FRANKLIN COVER

Sandy Abernathy
RUSSELL MORASH

Dr. Bobby Denton
JOHN DEVLIN

Bokonon
KEVIN MC CARTHY

Island Girl
EDIE LYNCH

Soldier
JERRY GERSHMAN

Dr. Paul Proteus
JAMES SLOYAN

Prosecutor
GEORGE SERRIES

Deaf Juror
ASHLEY WESTCOTT

Drunk
JOHN PETERS

Miss Martin
HELEN STENBORG

Dr. Hoenikker
HURD HATFIELD

General
DOLPH SWEET

Lead Caroler
HARRIET HAMILTON

Policeman
SAM AMATO

Diana Moon Glampers
BENAY VENUTA

First Stagehand
CARLTON POWER

Larry
JEAN SANOCKI

News Announcer
JACK SHIPLEY

Ballerina
ALEXIS HOFF

Harrison Bergeron
AVIND HAERUM

Short Order Cook
FRANK DOLAN

Nancy
SUSAN SULLIVAN

Lionel J. Howard
CHARLES WHITE

Announcer
PHILLIP BRUNS

Wanda June
ARIANE MUNKER

Hitler
PAGE JOHNSON

Cemetery Gardener
MC INTYRE DIXON

This book is based on the
television script of the
NET Playhouse production,

Between
TIME
and
TIMBUKTU

A SPACE FANTASY

Kurt Vonnegut, Jr., was
commissioned to be an advisor
on and contributor to the script
in 1971 and the program was first
aired nationally on public
television stations on March 13,
1972. Many good people created
funny stuff as the filming
progressed, most notably Bob
Elliott and Ray Goulding, and
Fred Barzyk, the director. The
first draft of the script, most
of which survived, was by
David O'Dell.

Preface

This book is said to have been written by me. And I *did* write it, too, pretty much—over the past twenty-two years. But it would never have occurred to me to put my words in this particular order. That vision was received by some friendly people at National Educational Television in New York and at WGBH in Boston. With my permission, they took unrelated incidents from several of my stories, and they tacked them together to form a rough draft of a script for a ninety-minute TV show.

I was reminded of the bizarre surgical experiments performed in the H.G. Wells tale *The Island of Dr. Moreau*. Dr. Moreau cut up all sorts of animals—and he assembled grotesque new creatures from the parts.

I began to fool around with the script myself. I grafted the head of a box turtle onto the neck of a giraffe, so to speak—and so on. Amazingly, chillingly, hilariously, the impossible creature lived for a little while. It was clumsy, funny-looking, and almost pathetically eager to please.

It had a soul, too, which was mainly supplied by an extraordinarily gifted actor my own age, William Hickey. Bill played the part of the reluctant astronaut, Stony Stevenson. Since Stony was not a strongly motivated character, and since we weren't sure what he was supposed to represent anyway, we asked Bill to be himself. He demonstrated that Bill as Bill, adrift in time and space, was an enchanting human being.

Hello, Bill.

My father loved the music of Kurt Weill, and he said one time, admiringly, that the music sounded as though it were written by an inspired amateur. My father was a professional architect. I think he came to resent the neatness and tightness and slickness which his professionalism (and his clients) imposed on his designs. He could never be slapdash or childish or passionately crude. He could never do what inspired amateurs did, which, among other things, was to leave a lot to Lady Luck.

This script, it seems to me, is the work of professionals who yearned to be as charming as inspired amateurs can sometimes be. True, we hired the finest actors and technicians we could find. As for the meaning of the show, though, we left that to Lady Luck. She was good to us this time.

We shot first and asked questions afterwards, which is the American way. It was a picnic. It was a lark. I have never had more skilful, amusing associates.

While we were filming the show, usually on weekends, I told other writers, "Hey, get into non-commercial television." I said this only to writers who were rich. "The pay is lousy," I said, "but the freedom is total, as nearly as I can tell. They'll get you almost any actor you want, they'll break their necks to create any effect you want, and the writer has as much authority as Alexander the Great."

I still feel that way.

As for myself, though, I am not going to have anything more to do with film—for this reason: I don't like film.

I love National Educational Television. I love

WGBH of Boston, which had so much to do with
the making of this film. I love George Roy Hill and
Universal Pictures, who made a flawless
translation of my novel *Slaughterhouse-Five* to
the silver screen. I drool and cackle every time I
watch that film, because it is so harmonious with
what I felt when I wrote the book.

Even so—I don't like film.

Film is too clankingly real, too permanent, too
industrial for me. As a stingy child of the Great
Depression, I am bound to complain that it is also
too fucking expensive to be much fun. I get the
heebie-jeebies every time I hear how much it will
cost to fix a scene that doesn't work quite right.
"For God's sake," I say, "leave it just like it is. It's
beautiful! Leave it be!"

I have become an enthusiast for the printed
word again. I have to be that, I now understand,
because I want to be a character in all of my
works. I can do that in print. In a movie, somehow,
the author always vanishes. Everything of mine
which has been filmed so far has been one
character short, and the character is me.

I don't mean that I am a glorious character. I
simply mean that, for better or for worse, I have
always rigged my stories so as to include myself,
and I can't stop now. And I do this so slyly, as do
most novelists, that the author *can't* be put on
film.

Every deeply felt novel which has been turned
into a movie has, as a movie, seemed one
character short to me. It has made me uneasy on
that account. I suspect that the audience has been
vaguely uneasy, too—for the same reason.

The worst thing about film, from my point of view,
is that it cripples illusions which I have encouraged

people to create in their heads. Film doesn't create illusions. It makes them impossible. It is a bullying form of reality, like the model rooms in the furniture department of Bloomingdale's.

There is nothing for the viewer to do but gawk. For example: there can be only one *Clockwork Orange* by Stanley Kubrick. There are tens of thousands of *Clockwork Oranges* by Anthony Burgess, since every reader has to cast, costume, direct, and design the show in his head.

The big trouble with print, of course, is that it is an elitist art form. Most people can't read very well.

Well, so much for film as compared with print. As a friend said of another terrific theory of mine: "It has everything but originality."

I might as well say something about the filming of my play *Happy Birthday, Wanda June.* It was one of the most embarrassing movies ever made, and I am happy that it sank like a stone.

It was all the director's show, which is usually the case. So was *Slaughterhouse-Five.* That's fine, as long as the director is a great director. George Roy Hill is a great director.

I had nothing to do with the script of *Slaughterhouse-Five,* incidentally. That was the work of Steven Geller—and a good job it was. I didn't meet him until after the picture opened. He is a novelist, too, and I asked him which he liked best, writing novels or screenplays. He preferred novels by far, since they were wholly under his control.

I told him what Bill Hickey, my actor friend, had said to me about writing for the legitimate theater or the screen, in effect: "Be prepared to direct what you write, or forget it. If you're going to write something but not direct it, you'll be doing only half your job."

Which is true.

I would like to say something about American comedians: they are often as brilliant and magical as our best jazz musicians, and they have probably done more to shape my thinking than any writer. When people ask me who my culture heroes are, I express pious gratitude for Mark Twain and James Joyce and so on. But the truth is that I am a barbarian, whose deepest cultural debts are to Laurel and Hardy, Stoopnagel and Bud, Buster Keaton, Fred Allen, Jack Benny, Charlie Chaplin, Easy Aces, Henry Morgan, and on and on.

They made me hilarious during the Great Depression, and all the lesser depressions after that. When Bob Elliot and Ray Goulding agreed to work on this TV show, I nearly swooned. I would have been less in awe of Winston Churchill and Charles de Gaulle.

I wrote some of their jokes in this script, and they delivered them gracefully. But they also made up a lot of new stuff, even when the cameras weren't operating, which made me laugh so hard that I thought I would go through the rest of my life wearing a truss.

One of them said this about Stony Stevenson's mother: "She certainly has nice manners for a welfare deadbeat." When they were asked out of the blue what an astronaut's favorite food was out in space, there was no hesitation. The prompt answer was, "Dehydrated artichoke hearts." And so on.

Cheers.

Between
TIME
and
TIMBUKTU

CONTEST ANNOUNCER

Good day, America. . . . At last, the day we're
going to announce the grand prize winner in the
Blast-off—Blast-off, as you know, the space food
of the astronauts—the Blast-off Space Food
Jingle Contest. Behind me, in this house, is the
winner. The winner does not know that he has
won the Blast-off contest. May I please have the
bottle . . . thank you, Miss Blast-off.

MISS BLAST-OFF

Here you are.

CONTEST ANNOUNCER
Lovely, lovely. Now . . . this is an exciting
moment. . . . I'm a little nervous, it's been so
many months. LADIES AND GENTLEMEN!
THE WINNER IS . . . Mr. Stony Stevenson,
12 Harrison Boulevard, Indianapolis, Indiana.
. . . AND NOW, MR. STEVENSON,
HERE WE COME!

[*Music up full*]

[CONTEST ANNOUNCER *knocks on door*]

CONTEST ANNOUNCER
Just think, ladies and gentlemen, in a few
moments from now in this typical modest
American home, in this modest American
community, you will meet the man who has won
the Blast-off Space Jingle Contest, the energy
drink of the astronauts and Mission Control.
We're going to present him with the grand prize, a
trip to the Chrono-Synclastic Infundibulum. Here
he comes now. . . .

MRS. STEVENSON
Yes?

CONTEST ANNOUNCER
Excuse me, madam . . .

MRS. STEVENSON
Oh, no thank you, we don't want any.

[MOM *starts to shut door.* CONTEST ANNOUNCER *knocks again*]

CONTEST ANNOUNCER
Madam, excuse me. . . . You don't understand. May I just speak to you for a moment? We are on network television right now.

MRS. STEVENSON
Oh!

CONTEST ANNOUNCER
Is this the home of Mr. Stony Stevenson?

MRS. STEVENSON
Yes. . . .

CONTEST ANNOUNCER
Well, may we see him please? We have a *very* important announcement.

MRS. STEVENSON
STONY!

VOICE OF STONY
WHAT DO YOU want, ma?

MRS. STEVENSON
SOMEBODY here for you. . . .

CONTEST ANNOUNCER
In a few moments, ladies and gentlemen, the magic of live television, the excitement . . . Here he comes now, here he comes. . . .

STONY

[*Quietly, meekly*]

Oh, hi.

CONTEST ANNOUNCER
Hello, good day to you. . . . You are Mr. S.
Stevenson?

STONY
Yes, that's right . . . Stony Stevenson.

CONTEST ANNOUNCER
Stony Stevenson, CONGRATULATIONS!
Pardon me, mama. We have an important
announcement to make to you right now. YOU
ARE THE WINNER, THE GRAND PRIZE
WINNER in the Blast-off Space Jingle Contest.
. . . AMERICA, HERE'S YOUR WINNER—
STONY STEVENSON!

[*Flashbulbs go off. March music starts up. Cheering crowd*]

[STONY *is led from the house to a car*]

MRS. STEVENSON
Stony!! Stony, come back!

[STONY *in car, looks back toward* MOM]

Between
TIME
and
TIMBUKTU

A SPACE FANTASY
BASED ON MATERIALS BY

Kurt Vonnegut, Jr.

GESUNDHEIT
This is Walter Gesundheit

WILLIAMS
and ex-astronaut Bud Williams, Jr.

GESUNDHEIT
bringing you every exciting moment of the Flight
of Prometheus-5, direct from Mission Control
Space Flight Center.

WILLIAMS
Right.

GESUNDHEIT
Three months ago Mr. Stony Stevenson received
the news on nationwide TV that he had won first
prize in the Space Poem competition.

WILLIAMS
Quite a thing.

GESUNDHEIT
Yes it is. And since then he has undergone one of
the most concentrated crash courses for
astronauts ever devised and in a very few
moments we will see the results of these endeavors.
Prometheus-5 with Astronaut Stony Stevenson

aboard is on the launching pad and with you we
will wait out the final moments before blast-off.

WILLIAMS
Really is tense here today, Walter. . . .

GESUNDHEIT
Right, Bud. Tense is the word of the hour as
Astronaut Stony Stevenson sits high atop the
rocket awaiting his launch into the Chrono-
Synclastic Infundibulum.

WILLIAMS
Walter, I understand we have contact with
Astronaut Stevenson in his capsule now. . . .
Why don't we find out just what he's thinking in
these last few moments before blast-off.

[*Cut to Rocket Ship sitting quietly on launching
pad*]

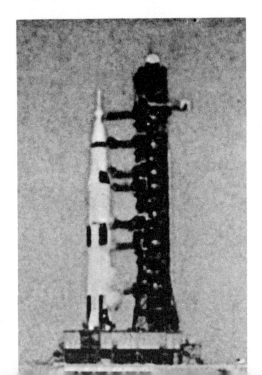

GESUNDHEIT

Good thinking Bud. . . . Come in Stony
Stevenson. . . . Astronaut Stevenson . . . this
is Walter Gesundheit and ex-astronaut Bud
Williams . . . can you hear us?

[*Long pause, then nothing but noise and
interference on the monitor*]

WILLIAMS

Can you hear him, Walter?

GESUNDHEIT

Can't even see him. . . . Sorry, it seems we have
some difficulty with the connection to the space
capsule. For those of you who just tuned in, the
countdown for the launch of Prometheus-5 has
been temporarily halted at zero minus sixty

seconds. Bud . . . you were on Prometheus-1 and Prometheus-3.

WILLIAMS

That's right, I was.

GESUNDHEIT

What I really wanted to ask was . . . how did a highly trained technical person like yourself feel when you learned that a man who writes poetry in his spare time was going to make this trip?

WILLIAMS

At first, I felt he would be too emotional, Walter. I thought, Maybe he can give us some fancy descriptions of things, but if the going really gets tough, the way it did on Prometheus-3 . . .

GESUNDHEIT

You mean, when the Tang got loose in the landing module . . . ?

WILLIAMS

There was Tang all over the place, and no gravity. But when I realized that they were going to put a man right through a time warp, a Chrono-Synclastic Infundibulum, I said, "Well . . . maybe only a poet could describe a thing like that."

GESUNDHEIT

Words somehow seem inadequate when one is describing space.

WILLIAMS

Yes, if you remember, I had a great deal of trouble describing Mars.

GESUNDHEIT
You said it looked like your driveway back home
in Dallas.

WILLIAMS
Yes, that's what it looked like to me at the time.
So, if they were to put me through a time warp—

GESUNDHEIT

[*Aside*]

A Chrono-Synclastic Infundibulum . . .

WILLIAMS
—right—I probably would be speechless myself.

GESUNDHEIT
Um.

WILLIAMS
I mean . . . you put a man through a time warp—

GESUNDHEIT

[*Aside*]

A Chrono-Synclastic Infundibulum.

WILLIAMS
—and for a while he's going to be scattered not
only through space but time! He's going to be a
hundred places at once, and there's no way of
guessing just where, you know.

GESUNDHEIT
Bud . . . what kind of training has Astronaut

Stevenson gone through to prepare for this mission?

WILLIAMS
Walter . . . he's really trained very hard for the mission. You know we have a standard here at Mission Control . . . standard of excellence.

GESUNDHEIT
That's the atmosphere here at Mission Control, Bud . . . excellence.

[*Cut to flashing control panel. Truck past sea of wires and connectors. CU of finger pushing switch . . . word next to it says "Flush." CU of sweating brow. CU of eyes as they move from left to right.*]

WILLIAMS

It takes a special person, one with fortitude . . .
ambition, skill, intelligence, forthrightness,
awareness, and most of all guts to work here in
the heart of Mission Control. It's here that the
very life of Astronaut Stevenson will be watched
over and cared for, where his every heartbeat,
respiratory and digestive activity will be monitored
by computer. Excellence is the byword and the
product of this crack team here at Mission Control.

GESUNDHEIT

I understand that we have now made contact
with Stony Stevenson high atop his launch rocket.
Hello, Stony.

[*A lot of noise and a vague picture of Hopalong
Cassidy riding across the screen of the monitor,
then more noise*]

GESUNDHEIT

Yes, and it takes a special kind of a man to be a
space adventurer, an explorer of the unknown, a
man from Mission Control is very special indeed.

[*Music, rich and full*]

Geologist.

Physicist.

Electrical Engineer.

Physician.

Chemist.

Test Pilot.

The Air Force.

The army and the navy.

And now the poet, Stony Stevenson.

One and all, the great team . . .

THE
MEN
FROM
MISSION
CONTROL

GESUNDHEIT

Before we hear from our astronaut we are
fortunate to have Mrs. Stevenson, Stony's mother,
with us in the studio. She has been keeping up a
constant vigil here at Mission Control. Bud . . .

WILLIAMS

You must be very proud of your son.

MRS. STEVENSON

It doesn't seem possible. Nobody in our family
ever won a contest.

WILLIAMS

Well, I'd like to announce to you and to the American public that Stony was made an honorary private in the United States Army this morning.

MRS. STEVENSON

Isn't that something!

WILLIAMS

Isn't that great?

MRS. STEVENSON

Uncle George won't believe it . . .

WILLIAMS

When he was a child, did you have any intimation that someday he would be going off into space like this?

MRS. STEVENSON

He used to be interested in the pressure cooker. He would get it out and play with it, seal it up tight, and then unseal it again . . . put different things in it . . . marbles, his toy fire engine. . . .

WILLIAMS

Um.

MRS. STEVENSON

Now they got *him* all sealed up.

WILLIAMS

I was about to say that he came from a typical American family, but of course he's not a typical American astronaut, is he?

MRS. STEVENSON

Depends on what kind of typical you're talking
about. I think we're typical Americans. His father
committed suicide. I've been married three times
. . . happily only once.

WILLIAMS

To Stony's father.

MRS. STEVENSON

To Fred K. Bonzer.

[*Silence*]

WILLIAMS

Stony did grow up, though, in the American
Middle West . . .

MRS. STEVENSON

Indianapolis.

WILLIAMS

In what we could consider a typical Hoosier
house . . .

MRS. STEVENSON

The welfare people had us in a Holiday Inn for a
while. That was quite a scandal.

WILLIAMS

Why do they call people from Indiana Hoosiers?
I've often wondered about that.

MRS. STEVENSON

Nobody knows.

[*Silence*]

WILLIAMS
So Stony Stevenson's roots are in Indiana soil.

MRS. STEVENSON
He has a cemetery lot in Brooklyn, New York.

WILLIAMS
Pardon me?

MRS. STEVENSON
Fred K. Bonzer, my third husband, inherited a
cemetery lot in Brooklyn from a rich uncle. He
gave it to Stony on Stony's eighth birthday. . . .

WILLIAMS
Um.

[*Silence*]

MRS. STEVENSON
At a big party at the Holiday Inn.

WILLIAMS
Um.

MRS. STEVENSON
That was before the newspapers found out the
welfare people had put us up there at thirty bucks
a night.

WILLIAMS
Right.

MRS. STEVENSON
That was just before the
  [*Bleep*]
hit the fan.

WILLIAMS

Are you signaling me, Walter?

GESUNDHEIT

Sorry to interrupt, Bud. Let's switch now to
Colonel Donald "TEX" Pirandello, the voice of
Prometheus-5. Tex, I know there's been a lot of
conversation about will he wear his space suit or
won't he. Do you have a final decision on that?

[TEX *at mission control desk*]

TEX

Right, Walter . . . soon after launch he will take off his outer protective envelope or space suit and eject it from the capsule. He will not need his space suit in his travels. . . . Astronaut Stevenson will drink orange-flavored hydrogen peroxide, and absorb the slowly released oxygen through the wall of his small intestine. Communications between the capsule and Mission Control will be established momentarily. In the meantime, I know he would want me to let everybody know how happy and proud he is today. He's raring to go. We are at sixty seconds and counting.

GESUNDHEIT

Oh, my.

[*Nervous laugh*]

We interrupt this countdown to bring you special coverage of a disturbance at South Gate. Take it away, Sandy.

[*Scene changes to* SANDY *at south gate in crowd of protestors*]

SANDY ABERNATHY

This is Sandy Abernathy at the South Gate of
Mission Control. The radical evangelist Dr.
Bobby Denton and a group of his avid followers
are protesting the launching of Prometheus-5 It's
an angry crowd and the guards cannot hold . . .

TEX

Minus forty-five seconds.

SANDY ABERNATHY

Dr. Denton was just released yesterday from
federal prison where he had served a nine-day
sentence for disorderly conduct for his actions at
the Poor People's March last June.

WILLIAMS

Thirty seconds and counting.

SANDY ABERNATHY
They have refused to leave. Let's take a listen.

DENTON
These scientists, I say, are just building another
tower of Babel. We don't need them and we
don't need their countdowns to get us where we're
going, do we?

CROWD
No!

DENTON
Because we have our own countdown here on
God's green spaceship. You know what it is?

CROWD
No!

DENTON
Do you want to hear it?

CROWD
Yes!

DENTON
TEN!

VOICE FROM MISSION CONTROL
Ten . . .

DENTON
Do you covet thy neighbor's things?

CROWD
No!

VOICE FROM MISSION CONTROL
Nine . . .

DENTON
Nine! Do you bear false witness?

CROWD
No!

VOICE FROM MISSION CONTROL
Eight . . .

DENTON
Eight! Do you steal?

CROWD
No!

VOICE FROM MISSION CONTROL
Seven . . .

DENTON
Seven! Do you commit adultery?

CROWD
No!

VOICE FROM MISSION CONTROL
Six . . .

DENTON
Six! Do you kill?

CROWD
No!

BUD and WALTER
Five . . .

DENTON
Five! Do you honor thy father and mother?

CROWD
Yes!

TEX
Four . . .

DENTON
Four! Do you keep the Sabbath?

CROWD
Yes!

TEX
Three . . .

DENTON
Three! Do you take the Lord's name in vain?

CROWD
No!

BUD and WALTER
Two . . .

DENTON
Two! Do you make any graven images?

CROWD
No!

TEX
One.

DENTON
BLAST-OFF!

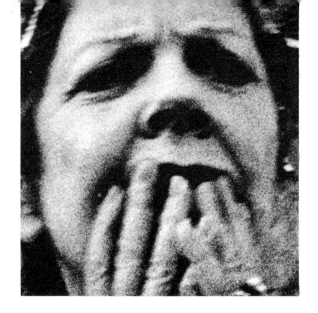

MRS. STEVENSON
Oh!! Blast-off!!

[*Cut to Rocket Ship sitting quietly on the launching pad . . . nothing happens, then . . .*]

GESUNDHEIT

Blast-off.

VOICES FROM MISSION CONTROL

Absolutely no reading . . . No . . . That's it.
Hold it. . . . All right.

[*Rocket Ship blasts off*]

TEX

It's all systems go. . . . Prometheus-5 has
cleared the tower. . . . It's a good one . . .
delta acceleration at maximum . . . optimum
burnout projected . . . cabin tracking locked in
. . . looks good from here.

GESUNDHEIT

Well, there you had it . . . the successful launch
of Prometheus-5, a historic day as man reaches
farther into space to find the meaning of life.
Traveling at twenty-eight thousand miles an hour
Stony Stevenson is headed for the Chrono-
Synclastic Infundibulum. And it is in that time
warp where Astronaut Stevenson may find the
answer to all creation.

*[Scene changes to celebration at Mission
Control. Chorus sings "For He's a Jolly Good
Fellow." Noises of celebration, champagne
flowing]*

GESUNDHEIT (*Voice Over*)
What did you think of Astronaut Stevenson and
the launch of Prometheus-5, Bud?

WILLIAMS (*Voice Over*)
Well, I thought he did real fine, Walter, and this
launch certainly couldn't be called a lemon . . .
no, sir . . . it's no lemon.

WILLIAMS
They're really having a great time, aren't they?

GESUNDHEIT
They're really pleased.

WILLIAMS
They deserve it, too.

GESUNDHEIT
Really pleased.

GESUNDHEIT

[*Laughs*]

They're really pleased.

WILLIAMS
They deserve it.

[*Chorus sings "For He's a Jolly Good Fellow."*]

GESUNDHEIT

[*Laughs*]

We could stand some of that bubbly ourselves.

[*Staff of mission control make a toast to* STONY. *Music up. Dissolve to lonely Rocket Ship in space*]

TEX

All indicators point favorably. Respiration, heartbeat, blood pressure, oxygen, water, cabin pressure, all indicate A-OK.

STONY

[*Quietly, emerging from shock*]

Then, I'm not dead . . .

TEX

Oh, no—you're just fine . . . you're just fine. We do get an excess moisture reading for the upper module of your space suit.

STONY

Yeah. Me, too.

TEX

You have a simple explanation?

STONY

Yeah.

TEX

Could we have it, please?

STONY

I think I threw up.

TEX

[*Laughs*]

Hey, o dog-gone it, we've lost him.

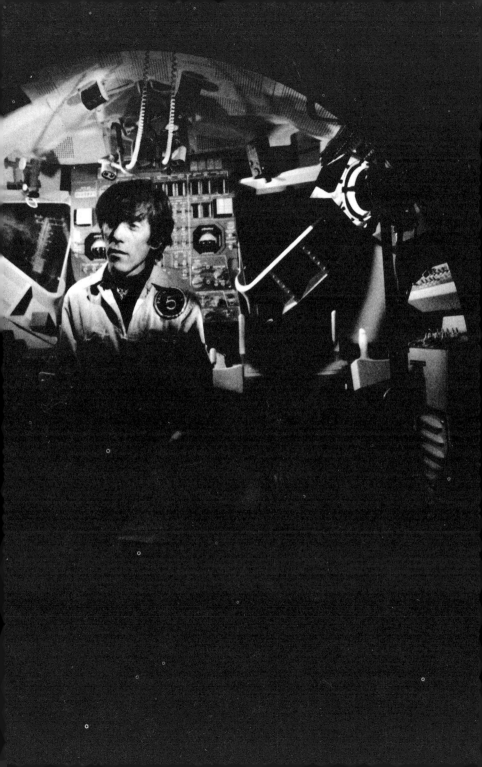

JULY

[*Music up, then fades slowly*]

TEX
You have one hundred and twenty million miles
to travel and according to latest calculations you
should reach the Chrono-Synclastic Infundibulum
in three months, four days, thirteen hours, three
minutes, and seven seconds.

[*Music up again, then fades*]

MRS. STEVENSON
Stony . . .

STONY
Ma? Is that you? It's good to hear a familiar
voice, ma.

MRS. STEVENSON
You're a very brave boy, Stony. I'm very proud of
you . . . and so is your Aunt Alice, and Cousin
Bruce. Mrs. Meyers from next door says you
come to dinner when you come back from your
trip.

STONY
That's real nice of her, mom.

GESUNDHEIT

I see Mom Stevenson's still in Mission Control,
Bud.

WILLIAMS

That's right, Walter. She's moved right in.

GESUNDHEIT

A mother standing by her son in his moment of
need.

WILLIAMS

She's moved a cot in the back of the retro
readouts and she's put doilies on the backs of all
the chairs.

GESUNDHEIT

A marvelous woman, Bud.

[*Music*]

TEX

You want to tell us if you plan to write any more poetry?

STONY

Yes, my first one is going to be a sestina, I hope.

TEX

Well, a sestina. All I know about poetry is Burma-Shave.

STONY

A sestina has six stanzas with six lines each . . . and the same six words and the lines of every stanza, you see, but in different order each time. The six words I've chosen are taken from man's words when he set foot on the moon: "One, long, step, for, man, kind." The order of the end words in the second stanza will be, "Long, one, man, kind, step, for." And then in the third stanza it is to be, "For, step, kind, man, one, long." In the fourth stanza it will be "Step, kind, for, one, long, man."

50

SEPTEMBER

OCTOBER

NOVEMBER

GESUNDHEIT
Merry Christmas, this is Walter Gesundheit . . .

WILLIAMS
and Bud Williams, Jr.

GESUNDHEIT
bringing you the continuing saga of Prometheus-5.
Private Stony Stevenson is approaching the core
of the time warp at a speed of twenty-eight
thousand miles an hour.

Silent Night
Holy Night . . .

TEX

He's fading . . . he's fading . . . I've lost him,
I've lost him.

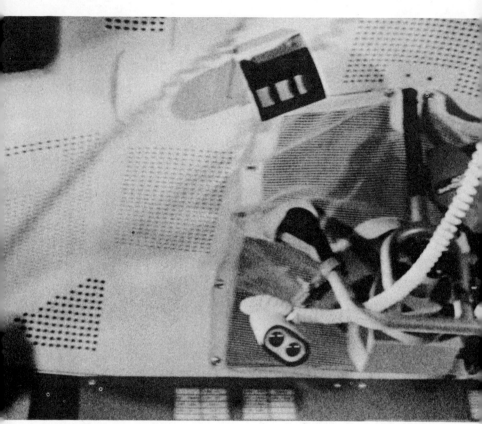

GESUNDHEIT

It is now six months since Stony Stevenson
blasted off on his epic adventure. Communications
have become increasingly hard the farther he
moves away from earth. But the moment has
arrived by all our calculations when Stony will
hit the Chrono-Synclastic Infundibulum. . . .

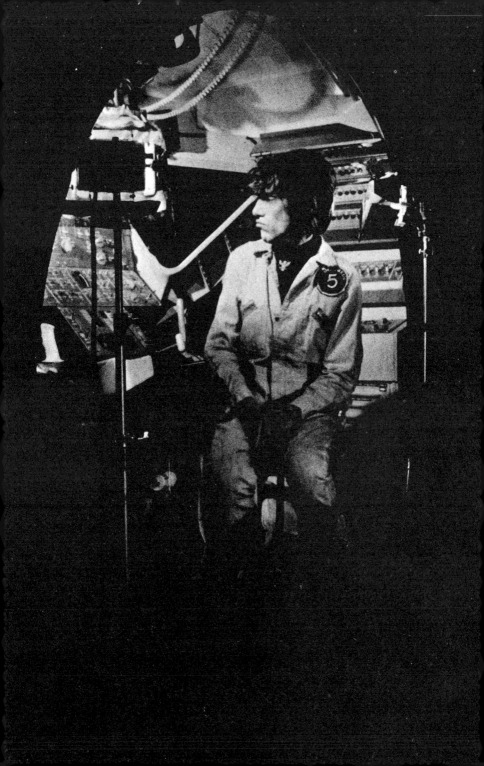

GESUNDHEIT

He could be anywhere and everywhere. . . .

[*Rocket Ship falls faster and faster, breaking
into flames. We hear a faint scream. Colors
. . . Swirls . . . Blobs moving and dancing
. . .* STONY *flapping arms, distorted as if his
molecules were disorganized.* STONY *six images
run across the screen . . . three in sync and
of different colors and the other three out of
sync, but also in various colors. Music . . .
Dixieland dance piece.* STONY *emerges again
. . . this time doing a dance with himself.*]

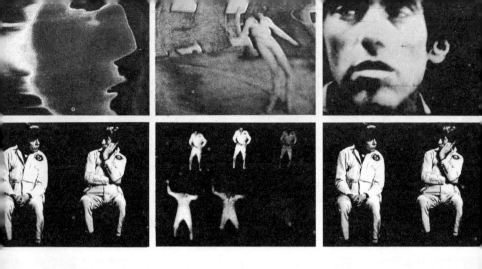

STONY I
Who are you?

STONY II
I was just going to ask you the same thing.

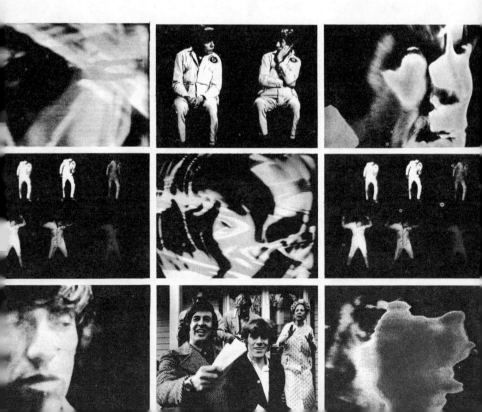

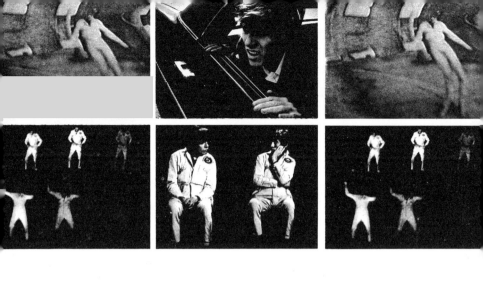

STONY

This is a mistake. . . . Oh, what a terrible mistake.

MRS. STEVENSON
Stony, can you hear me? Can you hear me, son?
This is mother.

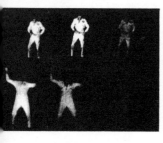

STONY I
Did they tell you to expect this?

STONY II
They told me I might come straight back to earth
in the present or the future, not the past.

STONY I
The past, the past . . . oh, the past . . .

GESUNDHEIT
I guess nobody knows now when we'll see
Corporal Stevenson again.

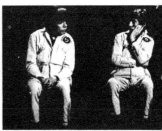

WILLIAMS
No, if ever . . .

[Picture goes black, then find body of STONY
laying on beach on the Island of San Lorenzo]

STONY
Am I dead yet?

GESUNDHEIT

I understand that Stony's writing a poem out there in space, Bud.

WILLIAMS

Oh, really?

GESUNDHEIT

Yes, and he's chosen those immortal words first spoken by man when he stepped on the moon.

WILLIAMS

Those words are very patriotic, Walter.

GESUNDHEIT

"One step for man . . ."

WILLIAMS

No, I think it was, "A giant step for man, a long leap for mankind."

VOICE OF STONY
Am I dead yet?

WILLIAMS

"One long step for mankind . . . ?"

GESUNDHEIT

No, it was, "One step onto the moon for
man . . ."

WILLIAMS

"Moon" wasn't in there, Walter. Not in that . . .

GESUNDHEIT

"One step"—wasn't it?—"for man, and two steps
for mankind."

WILLIAMS

"One step for man, and two steps for mankind?"
It doesn't flow the way it did originally.

GESUNDHEIT
"I'm stepping now for man . . ."

WILLIAMS
I think you have it now.

GESUNDHEIT
". . . hoping that all mankind will remember
this moment . . ."

WILLIAMS
". . . in history."

GESUNDHEIT
Did he say "two steps" at all?

WILLIAMS

No, it was, "One step for man and one for mankind." I . . . does anybody . . . ?

[STONY *is welcomed by people of San Lorenzo*]

BOKONON

Welcome to the island of San Lorenzo. Does that
make you happy or sad?

STONY

[*Looking around*]

That depends, I suppose.

BOKONON

A wise answer. We fished you from the sea. Are
you all right?

STONY

I think so.

BOKONON

Good.
Allow me to introduce myself—I am Bokonon,
author of the *Books of Bokonon*.
These are some of my pupils.

STONY

My name is Stevenson. Call me Stony.

BOKONON

I am very interested to meet you. I suspect we may belong to the same karass. You see, I myself was washed ashore on this island forty-seven years ago. It was the major *vin-dit* of my *sam ah ki bo.*

[BOKONON *holds up book in his hand*]

I see you are not a Bokononist. Come, I will teach you.

[*Music, band, and voices singing a calypso number*]

Tiger got to hunt,
Bird got to fly,
Man got to sit and wonder,
Why, why why?

Tiger got to sleep
Bird got to land
Man got to tell himself
He understand.

BOKONON

The people, these children of mine, are practicing *bakomaru,* a gentle form of lovemaking . . . nonviolent lovemaking. Be happy, my children . . . Bokonon is watching over you.

BOKONON

We Bokononists believe that humanity is organized
into teams, teams that do God's will without ever
discovering what they are doing. Such a team is
called a karass. You are here, doing God's will,
not knowing exactly why you are doing it. . . .
You and I are members of the same team . . .
the same karass. Welcome to the team.

STONY

Thank you.

BOKONON

When I was washed ashore on this island, I found
a people almost crushed by poverty and political
repression. Now, I have given them a religion of
harmless lies, and you can see how happy they are.

STONY

How can a useful religion be founded on lies?

BOKONON

When the truth of your life is too terrible, that truth becomes your enemy.

[*Noise of helicopters*]

STONY

[*Running and yelling*]

What is it?

BOKONON

[*Plowing through underbrush*]

I forgot to tell you, my religion has been outlawed. The government is trying to kill me.

Don't worry. It happens all the time.

[*Natives are pursued—narrowly escaping from the invaders*]

SOLDIER

Come on now, where are you? Come on, where'd everybody go? I think we got 'em on the run now. Where are you guys hiding? Ugh, first I get mosquitoes and then I lose . . .

BOKONON

All right, my children. I think we're safe for the
moment.

[STONY, BOKONON *and girl native hide in bush*]

STONY

[*Still whispering*]

Excuse me, Mr. Bokonon. Why is your religion
outlawed?

BOKONON

It was my own idea. I thought it would give the
religious life of the people more zest, more tang.
It did, in the beginning.

STONY

And then?

BOKONON

[*With a troubled scowl*]

The president was my friend. He agreed to play
along. It was like a game, really. We agreed the
penalty for practicing the religion would be death
. . . on the hook.

STONY
Um.

BOKONON
No one was supposed to be killed. It was all
threats and rumors. And then . . . the president
and I drifted apart.

STONY
Were you very close?

BOKONON
He was my best friend. We had made a play, a
work of art, of our life on the island. He would
play the cruel tyrant in the city, and I the gentle
holy man in the forest. It was an innocent
make-believe—to distract the people from their
miserable existence. Everything was fine,
until . . .

STONY
Until people started really being . . . executed?

BOKONON

[*Nods sadly*]

Yes.

[Pauses for reflection]

[Sad music]

I suppose that it goes to show that you have to be
very careful what you pretend to be . . .
because one day you may wake up to find that's
what you are.

[*A swirling* STONY *image recedes into black oblivion*]

STONY
Oh—Oh!

VOICE OF ISLAND GIRL
He disappeared!

VOICE OF BOKONON
Yes . . . but I think he stayed as long as he could.

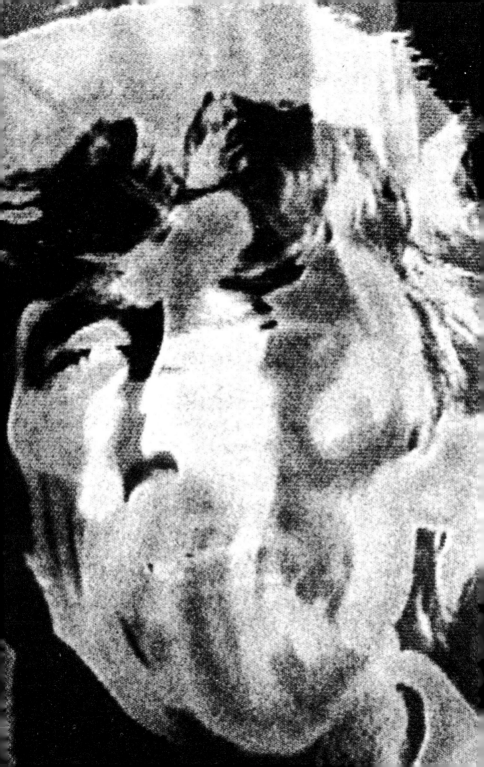

[*Back at Mission Control*]

GESUNDHEIT
"One step for mankind, and a . . ." That's
funny, I . . .

VOICE OF STONY
Wait! Will you wait?! Wait!

WILLIAMS
. . . my driveway reminded me of Mars.

GESUNDHEIT
Yeah.

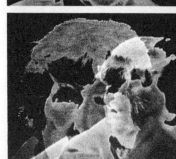

WILLIAMS

I don't think I ever pointed out that my driveway back home is red.

GESUNDHEIT

Well, that could be it then, right.

WILLIAMS

A lot of people have been kidding me about that, and I didn't point out that it is red.

GESUNDHEIT

I wasn't kidding you.

WILLIAMS

I know that, but we think of Mars as red, and that's why . . .

GESUNDHEIT

Well, let me ask you one thing. Was it a red driveway when you bought the house?

WILLIAMS

Yes, it's been red as long as I've known the place. It came that way. Quite a few in that neighborhood are red driveways, as a matter of fact.

GESUNDHEIT

Isn't that an unusual color for a driveway? I don't mean to harp on the subject, but—why don't you change it?

WILLIAMS

I had no particular reason to change it. I don't think we need to make a big point out of it.

GESUNDHEIT

No, I don't think it's very important.

[Slow fade on film shot of MAN
*running . . . long telephoto lens
. . . man starts walking fast . . .
then almost runs . . . breaks into
run . . . running as hard as he can,
running forever toward the camera
in desperation. Slow motion.*

*Overemphasized sound of his
breathing . . . as he runs faster it is
almost gasping. He is crying in fear
. . . We also hear heart beat.]*

PROSECUTOR

State versus Dr. Paul Proteus . . .
graduated after Second Industrial Revolution . . .
summa cum laude engineering and
   management . . .
rumored underground with revolutionary Gray
   Shirt Society . . .
captured last week attempting to destroy Illium
   control computer.

[*Voice echoes*]

You have pleaded guilty of conspiracy to commit
sabotage, to fomenting a riot, and to crossing
state lines unlawfully. Do you still deny you are
guilty of armed insurrection and treason?

[*Cut to gavel pounding . . . the sound echoes
forever . . . dissolve*]

[*Music*]

[*CU of wires being attached to skin. CU of pin
piercing skin. CU of electrodes put on finger.
CU of electrode attached to ear lobe. CU of
mike attached to heart area . . . bare
chested.*]

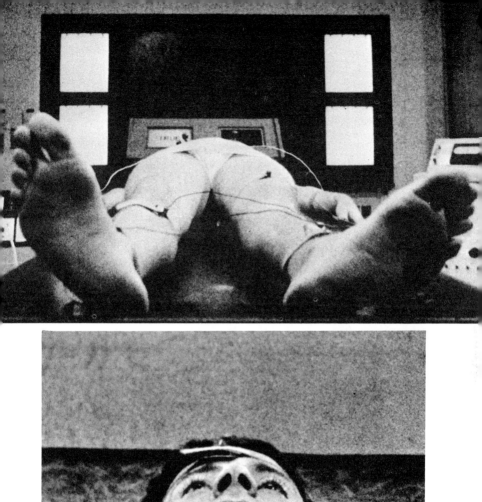

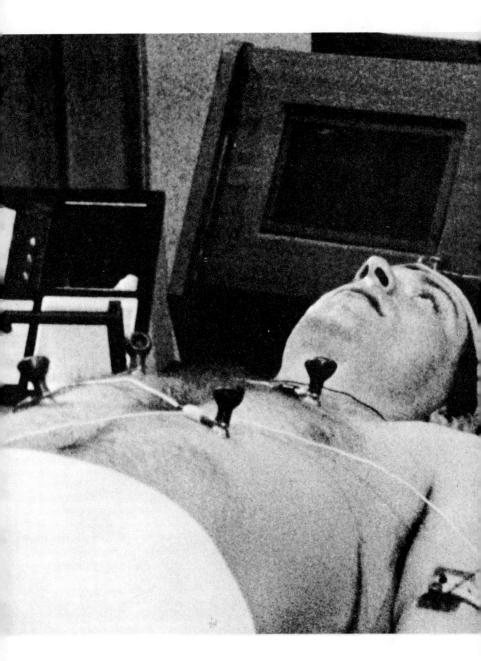

[*Defendant lies on a table strapped to electronic
lie detector gear. Jury stands with raised
hands,* STONY *among them*]

Do you solemnly swear in all causes between
party and party that shall be committed unto you,
you will solemnly render true verdict according to
the law and evidence, so help you God!

JURY
So help me God!

STONY
So help me God!

PROSECUTOR
You may sit down. . . . This use of force—you
don't regard that as levying war against your
country, as treason?

DR. PAUL PROTEUS
The sovereignty of a country resides in its people,
not in its technology. We are vigilantes, waging
war on a lawless technology in the name of the
people.

PROSECUTOR
Who are you anyway, a crackpot patriot or a
power hungry revolutionary?

DR. PAUL PROTEUS
I only want what's best for my country.

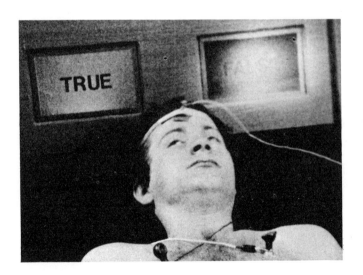

PROSECUTOR
A half-truth. What's the whole truth?

DR. PAUL PROTEUS
It is the truth.

[*Jury members are talking among themselves*]

PROSECUTOR
Quiet, quiet!

DR. PAUL PROTEUS
I demand an audit of this machine.

> [*Jury members break out into excited conversation*]

PROSECUTOR'S VOICE
Order, order. The court truth technician will please check the lie detector circuits.

STONY

Excuse me. Do you know what's going on here?
What is he yelling at him for? What did he do?
What century is this? Is this earth?

DEAF JUROR

   [*Wearing a hearing aid*]

You better ask somebody else. I miss a lot . . .
need new batteries.

STONY

Right . . . sorry.

DEAF JUROR

They ask me if I'm in favor of capital punishment,
but they don't ask if I hear or not.

   [*Laughs*]

STONY
Your Honor . . .

PROSECUTOR

[*Coming over to* STONY]

What's this?

STONY
Would you tell me the date, please, sir.

PROSECUTOR
Where's your gown? Didn't anybody tell you to
wear a necktie and a business suit and a gown
when serving on jury duty?

STONY

No, sir.

PROSECUTOR

If you appear tomorrow dressed like this, I'll hold you in contempt of court. We have a man on trial for his life here, and you come dressed like a member of the lower classes. How would you like to be tried by a member of the lower classes?

STONY

I'd hate it very much.

PROSECUTOR

Get a haircut!!!

STONY

Sir, won't you please tell me what date this is?

PROSECUTOR

Why would you interrupt the business of the court to ask a question like that?

STONY

I thought it might be my birthday.

PROSECUTOR

[*Shouts in disbelief*]

Your birthday?!!

DEAF JUROR

Birthday? I love birthdays!

[*Sings and jury members join in*]

Happy birthday to you, happy birthday to you.
Happy birthday dear juror . . .

PROSECUTOR
Quiet! Quiet! Now let's get down to business.
Lower the screen. Here is state evidence item
number thirteen.

[Screen is lowered behind defendant]

In this unbiased essay we will see the fruits of our
great society. This is the same society that the
defendant wishes to destroy. This is the same
society that is paying you for jury duty today. It
is indeed a land of plenty.

[An animated movie is shown]

ANNOUNCER
It's a good life, isn't it . . . John
Averageman? But did you ever stop to think
what makes it such a good life for you and
your loved ones? Well, the answer's easy—it's
modern technology and our industrial system.

JOHN
Those are pretty big words. What do they mean to me, an average guy?

ANNOUNCER
Well, John, perhaps I can show you. John, our
automated industrial system has made you
richer than Caesar . . .

Napoleon . . .

and Henry VIII put together.

Remember, for all his gold and armies Charlemagne could not have gotten one single transistor radio. Not to mention the insurance, health, and retirement benefits you get through your employer, John.

JOHN
I never looked at it that way. Gosh! Sort of
makes you think, doesn't it?

ANNOUNCER
But that's not all, John. Under this system our civilization has reached the dizziest heights of all time! Far beyond the wildest dreams of our past.

   [*The "Battle Hymn of the Republic" is heard, softly at first but slowly rising in volume*]

Thirty-one point seven times as many
television sets as the rest of the world put

together. Seventy-seven percent of the world's automobiles. Eighty-three percent of all the world's air conditioners.

[*Shouting now, to be heard above music*]

Eighty-five percent of its power lawn mowers.
Ninety-six percent of its helicopters.
Ninety-eight percent of its snowmobiles.

Ninety-nine point nine percent of the world's . . .

[*Voice drowned out by music*]

PROSECUTOR
Well, I hope the jury was paying attention to that.

[*Cut to* JURY . . . *Some sleeping, others knitting, some playing cards,* STONY *looking bored.*

Cut to JURY *as the green smoke starts to choke*
them . . . most of them screaming.

STONY *works his way past screaming old people*
. . . Bumps into the PROSECUTOR *who yells at*
him over the crazy sound of the machine
destroying itself and the Defendant screaming.]

Pull the plug . . . For Heaven's sake . . . pull
the plug . . . pull the plug.

[*Machine destroys itself in billows of green*
smoke. STONY *finds cord and trails it around in*
smoke and screaming people.]

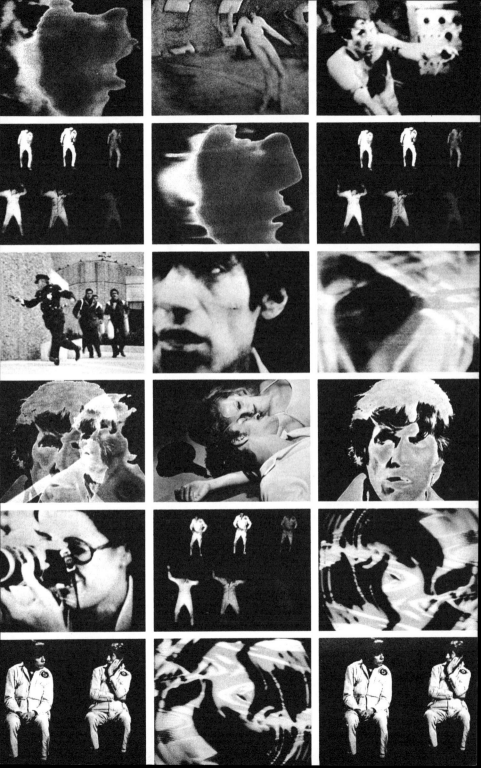

[*Scene changes to* STONY *on sidewalk asking for a dime. Only a drunk stops to listen.*]

STONY

Excuse me, excuse me. Could I have a dime for a phone call, please. Miss, excuse me, please . . . I wanted to ask you something. I'm an astronaut and I have to call Mission Control. You see, they thought of everything but a dime . . .

Could you spare a dime for a man who's been shot through a Chrono-Synclastic Infundibulum?

A DRUNK

[*Heartbrokenly*]

That is the saddest story I ever heard in my life.

[*He gives* STONY *all his change, spilling money all over the sidewalk.*]

That is the saddest story I ever heard in my life.

STONY
Thanks a lot. Thank you very much.

A DRUNK
Boy, oh boy. That is the saddest story I ever heard in my life.

[*Beginning to cry*]

That is the saddest story I ever heard . . . oh boy . . .

MAN FROM MISSION CONTROL
Hello.

STONY
Hi. Is Tex there, please?

MAN FROM MISSION CONTROL
Yeah. Just a minute.

   [*To* TEX]

Tex, Tex, it's for you.

TEX
Tex here. Hello, who is this?

STONY
Me. Stony Stevenson.

TEX
STONY! Where the hell are you?!!

   [*Mission Control staff starts talking excitedly*]

STONY
Well, it's . . . uh . . .

[*Spelling name on telephone box*]

S-C-H-E-N-E-C-T-A-D-Y. Oh! Schenectady. I'm in Schenectady.

[*Sudden panic at Mission Control as tracking system fails*]

EXCITED VOICES
Look! Something's gone haywire! Look! He's totally out of our tracking mechanism.

TEX
Private Stevenson!!

MAN FROM MISSION CONTROL
He's a corporal now.

TEX
Corporal Stevenson! This is an order. Everything

on Earth is completely off limits! Get back into
space!

STONY

Sir, I am not in control of my own destiny. It's a
miracle I can control my own bladder.

TEX

[*To Mission Control staff*]

Listen! He's lost control. Does anybody here
know how to get him back into outer space?

[*Excited babbling*]

Well, somebody better come up with a plan, and
soon!

[*To* STONY *again*]

Corporal Stevenson! Is there any way you can
get the hell out of there and back into outer space?

STONY

Sir, what happens happens. I think that I'm
traveling through my own nightmares . . . and
a few nice dreams, too. Otherwise, why would
everybody I meet speak English? Why else would
everything be so American, when America is all
I've ever known?

   Oh, sir, there *is* something strange to report about
Schenectady. I mean not that everything isn't
strange about Schenectady. It seemed to be
summer a minute ago, and now everything's
frosting up. Oh, there's another thing. I suddenly
feel very sleepy, sir. Sir, I . . .

[*As snow covers the phone booth,* STONY *yawns, has trouble keeping his eyes open and falls asleep. Scene changes to* STONY *asleep on surgical table in meat locker*]

DR. HOENIKKER

I really don't understand, Miss Martin. . . . How
could he have gotten in here?

MISS MARTIN

I really don't know Dr. Hoenikker. . . . It's a
total mystery.

STONY

[*Waking up*]

Mama?

HOENIKKER
Are you sure he's an extra body?

MISS MARTIN
I checked and checked . . . they are all
there . . . Truman Capote, Julius LaRosa,
Henry Kissinger . . .

HOENIKKER
When he's thawed, bring him in and we'll see if
we can find out who he is.

MISS MARTIN
Yes, doctor.

STONY
Mama?

MISS MARTIN
I'm not your mommy. All right, now. Sit up . . .
that's my baby.

STONY
Boy. What phone service in Schenectady . . .

MISS MARTIN
Don't be afraid. This is the Hoenikker Laboratory
of Immortality. Now stand up. That's the boy.

[*She helps him into a fur coat*]

Now that we've got you thawed out, we want to
keep you good and warm.

VOICE
Dr. Saroyan, please call extension 308 in the
sperm bank. Dr. Saroyan to the sperm bank
please.

[STONY *in wheelchair being pushed by* MISS
MARTIN]

MISS MARTIN
Upsy-daisy, here we go.

[Scene changes to HOENIKKER & GENERAL *in lab with bodies in bags]*

GENERAL

Doctor, you must do it. . . . It's important.
Dammit, Hoenikker, you know more about
freezing than any other human being in history.
I want you to figure out some way to freeze
battlefields, so American soldiers will never
again have to fight in mud.

DR. HOENIKKER

There's always winter, of course. A Russian winter
is especially good. Why don't you declare war
on persons who live in cold climates—Laplanders,
Eskimos, Finns.

MISS MARTIN

We are now going into Dr. Hoenikker's
laboratory. You mustn't be alarmed by what
you see here. Dr. Hoenikker has helped good
human beings who were about to die. He has
preserved them until cures can be found for their
diseases. He has frozen them into suspended
animation.

GENERAL

Listen, doctor, if you can get a handle on this I
can get you any amount of R and D money. We
can set up a crash program tomorrow. What do
you want? One million? Two million?

DR. HOENIKKER

So easy to get money for killing . . . and all I
can do is scrape up just two or three thousand
to freeze the best minds of our time.

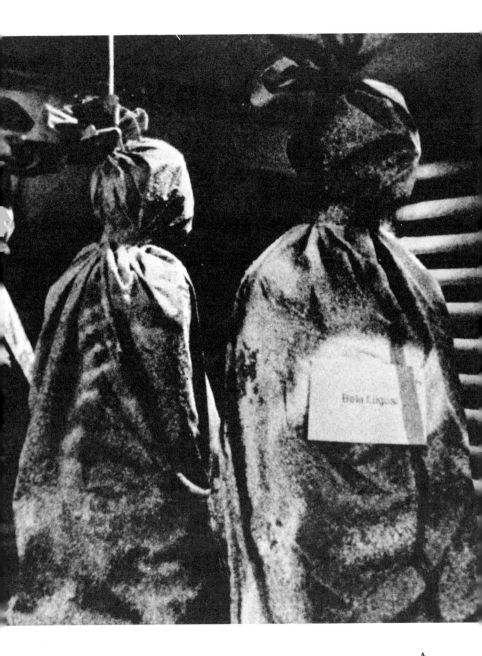

MISS MARTIN

Dr. Hoenikker is a wonderful man. He's very
busy, but he wants to ask you a few questions.
You're our mystery man, you know.

STONY

[*Moaning*]

Oh . . .

[MISS MARTIN *and* STONY *enter lab where*
HOENIKKER *and* GENERAL *are talking*]

GENERAL

OK, sure it is easy to get money for defense.
Damn right. Man is an infantry animal. There'll
always be wars and the winning side will be the one
who kills the most people on the other side.
And everybody likes to be on the winning side,
right?

DR. HOENIKKER

Um.

GENERAL

Right.

MISS MARTIN

Excuse me, doctor. Here we are.

DR. HOENIKKER

Ah, yes. Who are you?

STONY

The abominable snowman?

DR. HOENIKKER
Did you ever volunteer to be frozen here?

STONY
Not that I know of.

DR. HOENIKKER
Did you ever make a deposit in our sperm bank?

STONY
If I did, it was a small one.

[*Alarm bell*]

DR. HOENIKKER
What's that now?

MISS MARTIN
Oh, it's the girl pool.

GENERAL
The girl pool?

[*Girl pool enters singing "Joy to the World"*]

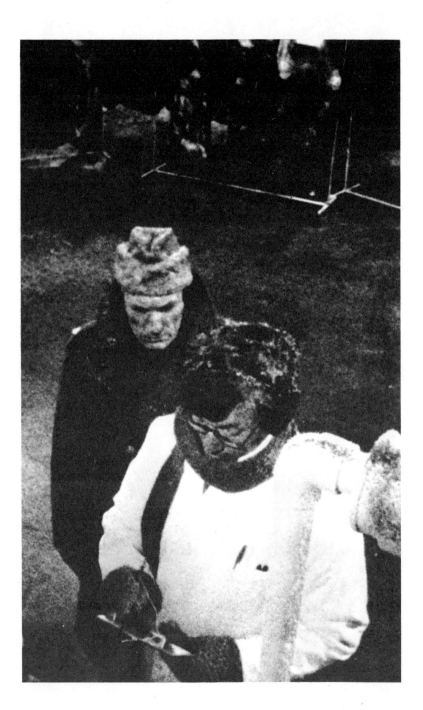

LEAD CAROLER

The girl typing pool from Building number three
wish you and yours a very Merry Christmas. From
Ann, Belinda, Joan, Glenda, Suzanne, and all the
girls in the typing pool.

DR. HOENIKKER

Merry Christmas.

[*Girl pool begins singing "O Little Town of
Bethlehem"*]

GENERAL

[*Whispers*]

Doctor, can we get back to the problem?

DR. HOENIKKER

I have been thinking about it. Now I suppose that
there are many ways in which water could freeze.
All ice forms, you see, around the nucleus, a seed,
we call it. Now suppose that there were one
seed with a melting point of say, a hundred and
forty degrees Fahrenheit. Now we would call that
Ice Nine.

[*Girl pool begins singing "Jingle Bells"*]

[*To girl pool*]

Oh, shush!

[*They continue, but very quietly*]

GENERAL

What's this got to do with my problem?

DR. HOENIKKER
You see general, a melting point of one hundred
and forty degrees makes anything below that hard
as a rock.

GENERAL
I'm beginning to see the point.

DR. HOENIKKER
Precisely. Mud.

STONY
Mud?

DR. HOENIKKER

The general wants to attack mud. It's the infantry's stickiest obstacle. Just picture the marines in a quagmire, a godforsaken swamp . . . with their trucks and tanks and howitzers all wallowing, sinking in stinking miasma and ooze. What do they do?

STONY

Use helicopters?

DR. HOENIKKER

Supposing one soldier had with him a tiny capsule containing a seed of Ice Nine. . . .

STONY

Ice Nine?

DR. HOENIKKER

[*Nodding head with enthusiasm*]

And suppose that soldier threw that tiny seed into the nearest puddle . . .

MISS MARTIN
The puddle would freeze.

DR. HOENIKKER
And all the muck around the puddle?

STONY

[*Not sure he has the right answer*]

Freeze?

DR. HOENIKKER
And all the puddles in the frozen muck?

GENERAL
They'd freeze!

DR. HOENIKKER
And all the pools in the frozen muck?

MISS MARTIN
They'd freeze!

DR. HOENIKKER
And all the streams in the frozen muck?

GENERAL

[*Shouting*]

They'd freeze!

DR. HOENIKKER

[*Shouting*]

You bet your bottom dollar they would.

STONY

[*Dismally, under his breath*]

Hooray . . .

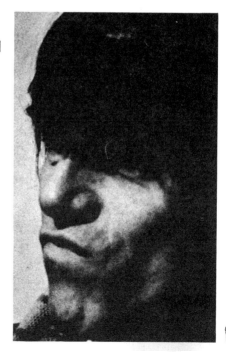

GENERAL
And the marines would rise from the swamp and
march on. That's it. That's just what I need,
doctor. Oh, wait'll the Pentagon hears about
this. It'll be the biggest thing since air transport.
. . . Merry Christmas, girls.

[*Girl pool choruses "Merry Christmas"*]

[*Girl pool exits singing "We Wish You A
Merry Christmas"*]

GENERAL
I'll let you know Monday how much I can finagle
for the pilot studies. You know, doctor, before
we're through, I've got a feeling that you're going
to turn out to be another Einstein.

[*General exits humming the "Marine Hymn"*]

[*Silence*]

STONY
There really isn't any Ice Nine, *is* there?

DR. HOENIKKER
Not yet.

STONY
I mean, if the streams were frozen in the swamp,
what about the rivers the streams fed?

DR. HOENIKKER
They'd freeze, too . . . but there is no such thing.

STONY
And the oceans the frozen rivers fed?

DR. HOENIKKER

[*Beginning to get angry*]

They'd freeze . . . what are you after, young man?

STONY
And the springs feeding the frozen lakes and streams, and all the water underground feeding the springs?

DR. HOENIKKER
They'd freeze.

STONY
And the rain?

DR. HOENIKKER
When it fell, it would freeze—

STONY
—into little hard hobnails of Ice Nine . . . and that would be the end of the world . . . .

DR. HOENIKKER
Damn it all, yes.

STONY
You should have told him that.

[STONY's *face distorts into a blue mask. His face rolls over itself again and again. Cut to Mission Control and the continuing television coverage.*]

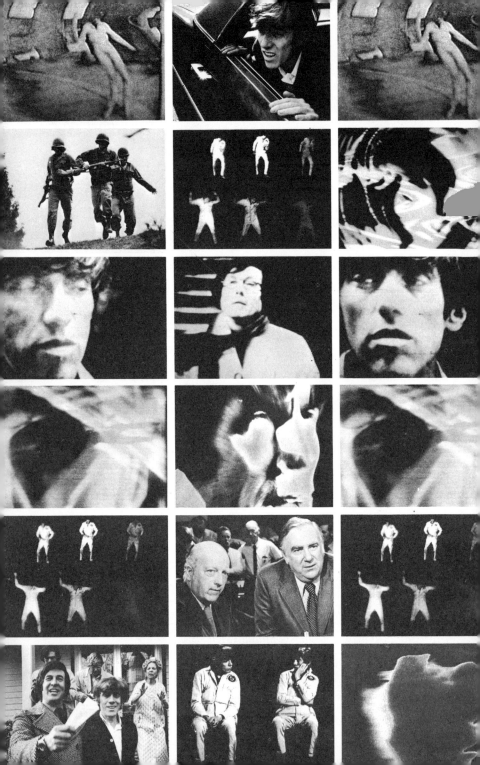

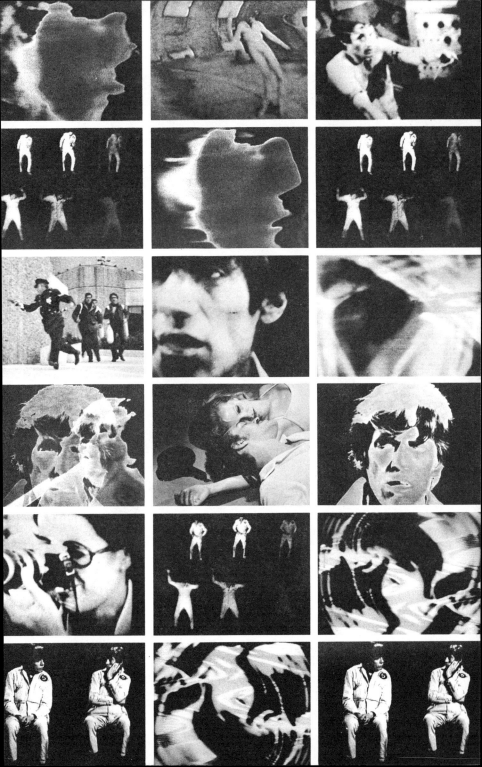

GESUNDHEIT
Due to the lull here in information from outer
space, Bud, right now . . . I was thinking you,
as our resident expert, could answer a few of the
questions that have been sent in here to Mission
Control from air viewers all over the country—

WILLIAMS

Sure thing, Walter.

GESUNDHEIT

—if we can prevail upon you for a few moments. This first one here is from little Susan, age ten, of Kenosha, Wisconsin. She says, "I love Stony. He is cute. Does he have a girl friend?"

WILLIAMS

No, I don't believe he does at the present time.

GESUNDHEIT

From San Francisco, Mr. R. L. says—asks, "When does Stony—" It appears to be incomplete.

WILLIAMS

"Shave," probably, is what he means. There is a time in the program once a day when we shave, just as there's a time to eat our meal, and so forth.

GESUNDHEIT

Well, now tell me, as long as you were out in space yourself, did you have any favorite foods?

WILLIAMS

Yes, dehydrated artichoke hearts were a favorite for me. The creamed turkey was very good, too.

GESUNDHEIT

And Tang . . .

WILLIAMS

Of course.

> [*Distorted image of* STONY *appears. A gun is pointed at him.*]

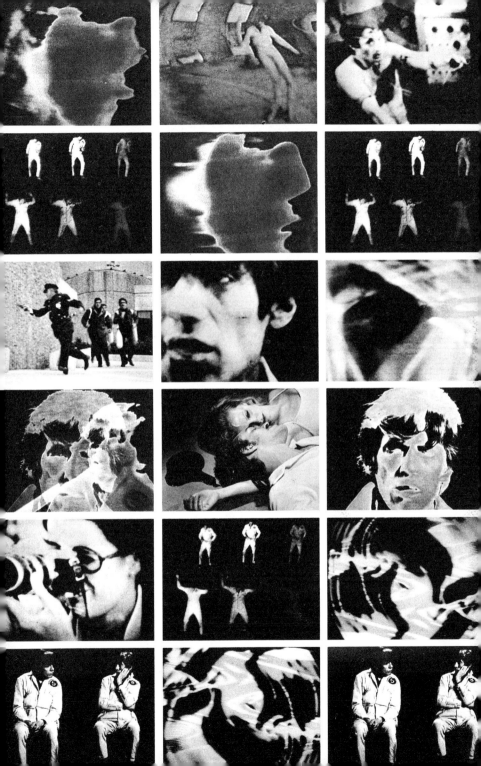

POLICEMAN

[*To* STONY]

Don't get smart, buster. I can pull a trigger as well as anybody.

[*Sound of gun. Gunshot hits fire alarm. Bells ring. Handicapped vigilantes chase* STONY.]

VOICE OF DIANA MOON GLAMPERS

Insist on your right to be equal! Under the two hundred and forty-third, and two hundred and forty-fourth, and two hundred and fifty-fifth amendments to our Constitution, it is the law of that land that nobody can be better looking than you are . . . nobody can be smarter than you are . . . nobody can run faster than you can . . .

DIANA MOON GLAMPERS

How do you do. I am Diana Moon Glampers,
your handicapper general. If you know of anyone
who can do something better than you can, it is
your duty to report that person to my office at
once. We want to handicap him fast, so he won't
make you or anybody feel inferior ever again.
Wherever you live, no matter what time of
day or night, simply dial one-seven-seven-six.
Tell the operator who it is that's making you feel
like something the cat drug in. We'll cream him.
We'll settle his hash.

[STONY *eludes his enemies. He finds himself trapped in a television studio.*]

FIRST STAGEHAND
Wow! Wh-wh-where's your ha-ha-ha-handicaps?

STONY
What?

FIRST STAGEHAND
G-g-g-g-g-et this g-g-guy some ha-ha-ha-handicaps!
G-g-g-get this guy some handicaps!

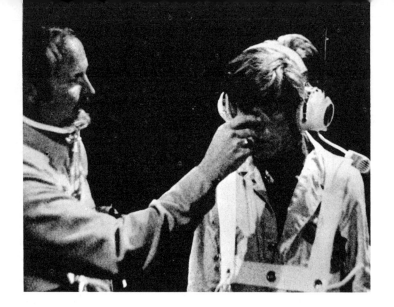

LARRY

Here you. Take this! Put it on and be quick
about it!

STONY

What is this? You're making a mistake. . . .

LARRY

You're one for the books, you are. . . .

FIRST STAGEHAND

Come on wise guy . . . into your handicaps.

[*They strap sandbags on* STONY]

LARRY

I've got two twenty-five pounders on the front,
Mike.

FIRST STAGEHAND

And two forty pounders on the back.

LARRY

That ought to slow you down, mac.

FIRST STAGEHAND

Hey, meathead . . . what's your IQ?

STONY

Oh, maybe a hundred and thirty-one.

LARRY

A hundred and thirty-one! Jeez, you gotta get a
radio! Mike, you got a spare?

FIRST STAGEHAND

Right . . . get it right away.

STONY

Why do I need a radio?

LARRY

Well, it's only fair, ain't it? I mean, it stands to
reason: you got more brains than most, so you
need a radio so you don't take advantage of
everybody.

[*Stagehand puts headsets on* STONY]

FIRST STAGEHAND

Here, put this on quick and you better get outta
here . . . here comes the director. . . .

[LARRY *puts false nose on* STONY]

LARRY

And wear this, too.

[*Awful noise hits headsets.* STONY *staggers with
the sound*]

DIANA MOON GLAMPERS

Anyone tampering with government IQ handicap radio will be subject to two years in prison or a fine of ten thousand dollars in compliance with article three-three-four-J. Hate that superior intellect of yours!

   [*Noise of headsets gets louder*]

That'll settle its hash!

   [STONY *throws off headsets. He hears tapping of* DIRECTOR'S *cane*]

STAGEHANDS

   [*To* DIRECTOR]

Good day, sir. Hello, Mr. Director.

   [*We see blindfolded TV* DIRECTOR *being led by seeing-eye dog*]

[*TV music up full*]

NEWS ANNOUNCER
And now direct from Television City, the home
of the big shows . . . we bring you . . .

[*Music swells*]

. . . Television City's Symphonette under the baton of Alfred Bluejean . . .

[*Music swells*]

. . . presenting Television City's own Corps de Ballet in a special performance of Musical Moments.

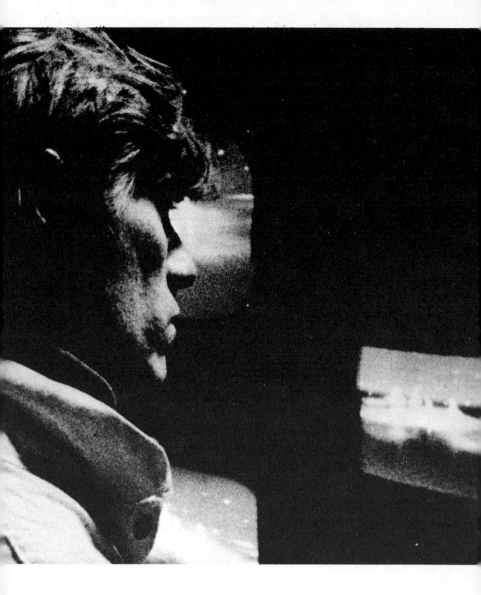

[STONY *gets rid of handicaps and hides in deserted television control room*]

[*Music is interrupted*]

NEWS ANNOUNCER

Good evening, ladies and gentlemen. This is a
. . . uh . . . We're interrupting this program
because of a . . . special news bulletin which has
just come in.

[*He looks for the bulletin*]

Ladies and gentlemen, the police have announced
today that Harry . . . Berger?

[*He removes thick glasses for a moment to read
name*]

Harrison Bergeron, age twenty-three, was being
held on . . .

[*Lifts glasses again*]

suspicion of conspiracy. Bergeron is a genius and
an athlete and is considered very dangerous.

[*Music resumes*]

NEWS ANNOUNCER
We had that story about Harrison Bergeron, and
we forgot to show you his picture. Here is a
picture of Harrison Bergeron, ladies and
gentlemen.

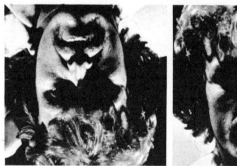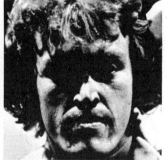

Harrison Bergeron is considered very dangerous.
So shoot first. That's all from the police. Good
evening.

[*Ballet resumes, but is interrupted by entrance of strange handicapped figure. It is* HARRISON BERGERON. *He breaks out of his handicaps.*]

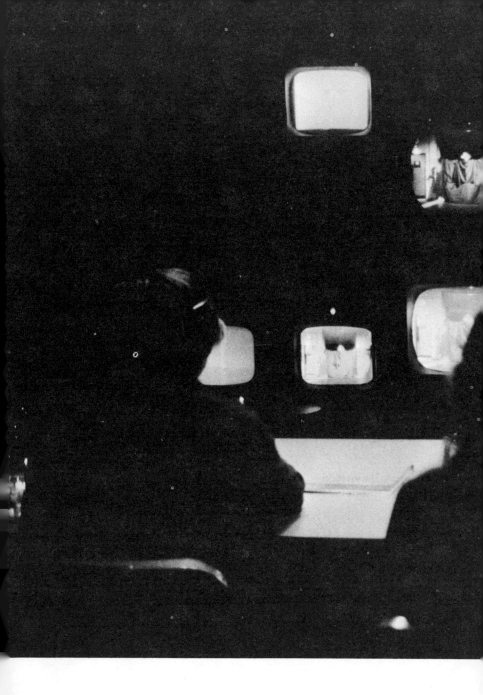

HARRISON BERGERON

[*To* BALLERINAS]

Who will dance with me?

HARRISON BERGERON
YOU!

VOICE OF TV DIRECTOR

[*On P.A.*]

This is your director speaking. I must advise you
to stop what you are doing. It is totally against
the law. I cannot be responsible for what happens
to you. Really, you must stop this immediately!
Won't you stop . . .

[HARRISON BERGERON *removes ballerina's handicaps*]

HARRISON BERGERON
Music!

[*The strains of "Romeo and Juliet" fill the air. They dance.*]

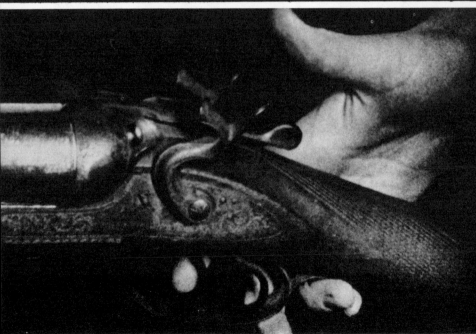

209

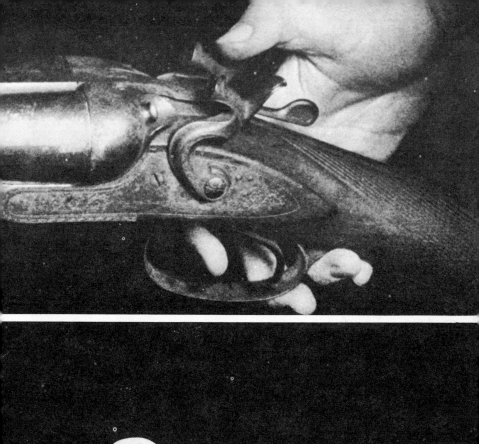

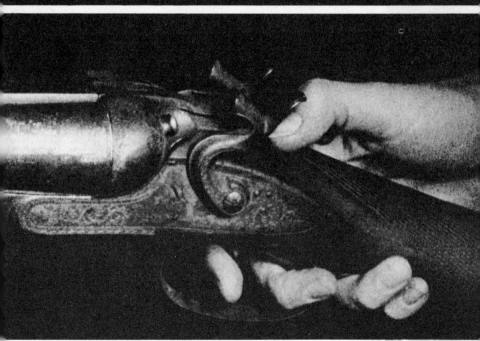

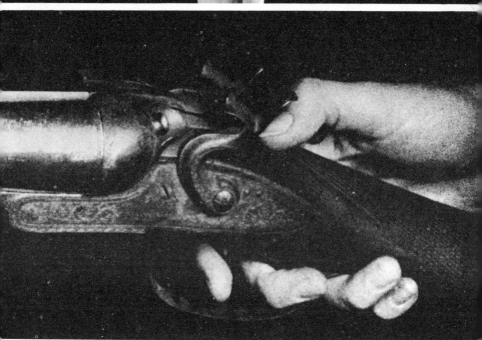

[Sound of rifle shot. The dancers fall in slow motion to the ground in a pool of blood. GLAMPERS *arrives carrying smoking double shotgun.]*

217

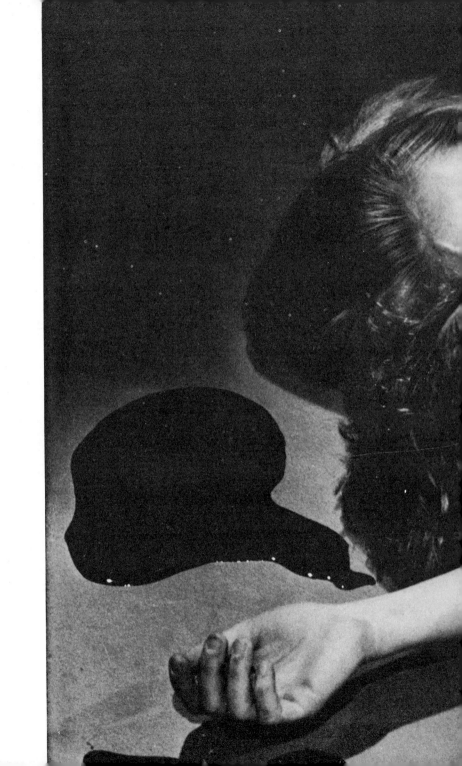

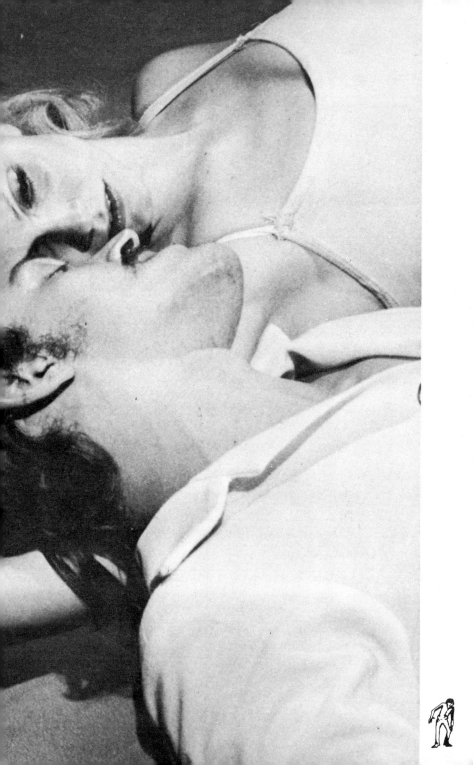

DIANA MOON GLAMPERS

Some of the TV shows they put on nowadays are
downright indecent!

[STONY's *image cascades through
an eternity of distortions.
Sad music fills the air.*]

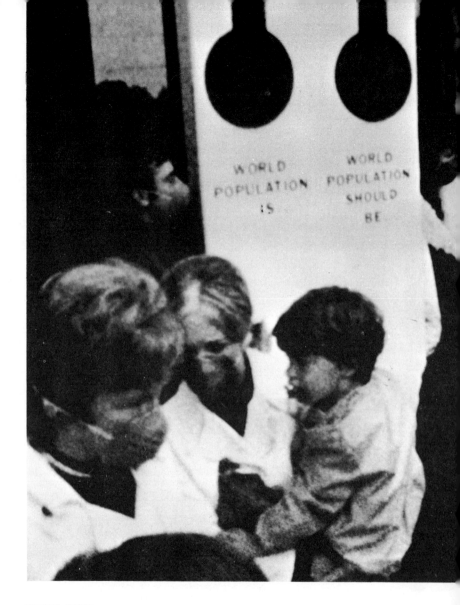

VOICE OVER

Forty-three billion babies were born last year.
The earth's population doubles every two months.
Eight million people die from suffocation every

day. If all the four-year-old children on earth
were placed end to end, they would reach the sun.
The oceans of the earth have shrunk to one-eighth
the size they were ten years ago. . . .

SHORT ORDER COOK

It's always stone cold by the time the client takes
the first bite. He isn't going to eat much more
than the first bite anyway. Appetite isn't a big
problem over there.

[*Indicating tray, which is ready*]

All right—take this over to—uh—

[*Checking the order*]

Howard—Mr. Lionel J. Howard.

STONY

Lionel J. Howard.

SHORT ORDER COOK

Don't worry about carrying disease. You're
carrying food to the Ethical Suicide Parlor. You
could have bubonic plague and it wouldn't make
any difference to the people over there. They'll
all be dead in an hour anyway.

[STONY *fights his way through throngs of people packed together like sardines. He enters a quiet motel-like establishment. He approaches a beautiful hostess who is rushing up the stairs.*]

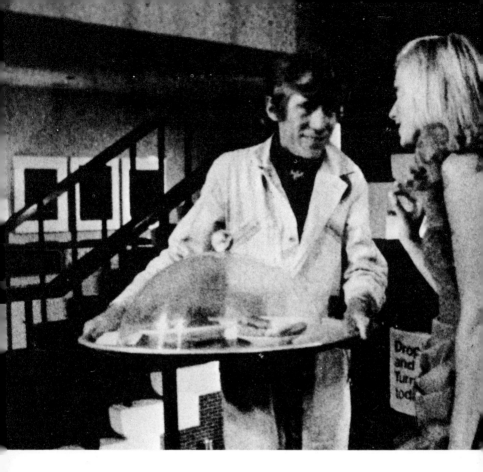

NANCY
You're late.

STONY
Sorry. I've got this—this thing about time.

NANCY
You're new.

STONY
Yes.

NANCY

You are not only late—but you are not smiling
enough. One ought never let that smile fade when
he is in here.

[STONY *smiles*]

Wider!

[STONY *smiles wider*]

Follow me.

STONY

What are all the people doing outside?

NANCY

What kind of a question is that? They're living.

STONY

Oh.

NANCY

Isn't any more crowded out there than it is anyplace else. You know anyplace that's any *less* crowded?

STONY

Nope.

NANCY

All right. Mr. Howard is right in there. You give him his meal, and you listen very politely to whatever he has to say. He's got a lot to say.

STONY

Can do.

NANCY

If he suddenly decides it's time to die, agree with him strongly—ring the bell, and keep him in a suicidal frame of mind till I get there.

STONY

Right.

NANCY

And smile . . .

[STONY *knocks on door*]

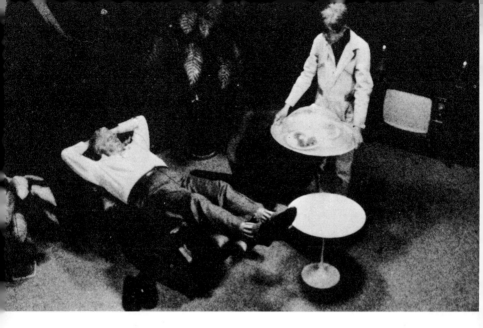

LIONEL J. HOWARD
Don't be shy. Come in! Come in! And wipe that
idiotic grin off your face. That's part of your job
—smile, smile, smile. You think I don't know that?

STONY
I brought your food.

LIONEL J. HOWARD
Put it on the table and sit down. Nice to get away
from the crowd. Think a lot of people would like
your job—the opportunity to get into a suicide
parlor without dying, but getting away from the
crowd.

STONY
I'm lucky, I guess.

LIONEL J. HOWARD
Human beings are like drupelets now.

STONY

Drupelets?

LIONEL J. HOWARD

The little knobs on a raspberry—those are drupelets. Now human beings are jammed together like that. What took you so long?

STONY

Just general ineptitude—some character flaws.

LIONEL J. HOWARD

Another two minutes of waiting for you, and I'd have walked out of here.

STONY

You would have decided to . . . to go on living?

LIONEL J. HOWARD

You call what they're doing out there living? I don't call that living.

STONY

There must be some other word.

LIONEL J. HOWARD

I've chosen cyanide. My wife wanted me to take the carbon monoxide, God knows why. "Maude," I said, "cyanide's more masculine." When they started the Ethical Suicide Program, I wrote the president of the United States and told him that veterans should have the option of being tied to a stake with full military honors and then shot with by a firing squad of United States Marines in dress blues. I got a form letter back. He said he'd passed on my suggestion to the VA. Wound up in some bureaucrat's wastebasket, I expect.

TV ANNOUNCER

Difficult to remember, isn't it? A day without
your ethical birth control pill. A day without that
wonderful numb feeling below your waist, a day
without . . .

STONY

What is that?

LIONEL J. HOWARD

Oh, the hostesses keep feeding those suicide
commercials in here. They're loaded with lots of
reasons to get the hell off earth.

TV ANNOUNCER

The beautiful pill that almost kept our population
in control. The beautiful pill that helps us
through the days—until the day of complete bliss
arrives—the bliss of blessed death. Just peace,
and your nearest Ethical Suicide Parlor. Your
favorite meal from Howard Johnson's . . .
served by our charming hostesses . . . in a
scrumptious suicide room, where you—and you
alone—can expire. Haven't you had enough? Why
don't you call your local Ethical Suicide Parlor
today? It's the ethical way to go.

LIONEL J. HOWARD

Been listening to that government stuff for years.
Never had any use for it before.

NANCY

You did say cyanide, didn't you, Mr. Howard?

LIONEL J. HOWARD

I've said a lot of things in this vale of tears.
Somewhere in there I must have said—cyanide.

NANCY

It's time.

LIONEL J. HOWARD

Could I see the suicide commercials again?

NANCY

Oh, Mr. Howard, you know these all by heart.

LIONEL J. HOWARD

You know, I once saw this experiment that the government ran to test the effectiveness of the ethical birth control pill, to see if a man who took one could feel anything below the waist. They blindfolded a guy and then gave him the Gettysburg Address. Right in the middle of the recitation they kicked him real hard, right where it hurts—and he never missed a syllable. I get to ask one last question.

NANCY

You what?

LIONEL J. HOWARD

I get to ask one last question, and you have to give me a truthful answer to it. That's the law.

NANCY

I never heard of that law. Oh, Mr. Howard, you're making that up.

LIONEL J. HOWARD

I swear it's the law.

NANCY

[*To* STONY]

A lot of 'em start making up new laws when it gets to be near the end.

LIONEL J. HOWARD

Why not?

NANCY

Mr. Howard, shall we ask for the needle now?

LIONEL J. HOWARD

If you'll answer my question.

NANCY

I'll make a bargain with you. You ask for the
needle. I'll give you the needle. Then you ask the
question, and I'll answer as best I can.

LIONEL J. HOWARD

All right. The needle, please.

NANCY

[*Withdrawing needle deftly*]

There you are.

LIONEL J. HOWARD

Yes sir . . . while he was reciting the Gettysburg
Address, they kicked him right in the ba . . .

[LIONEL J. HOWARD *groans softly, loses
consciousness*]

STONY

He—he never got to ask his question.

NANCY

Oh, that's all right. He'll wake up in about ten
seconds. He can ask it then.

[LIONEL J. HOWARD *stirs and looks toward*
STONY]

NANCY
I believe he wants to put the question to you.
You won't have time to answer.

[STONY *leans close.* LIONEL J. HOWARD *tries
again and again to phrase his question,
finally gets it out*]

LIONEL J. HOWARD
What . . . what are people—for?

[LIONEL J. HOWARD *dies*]

[*Dissolve to long line of candles quietly
flickering. The music is sad and slow.*]

[*Scene changes to* STONY *with kitten on flat dry
ground in wide empty arena at night*]

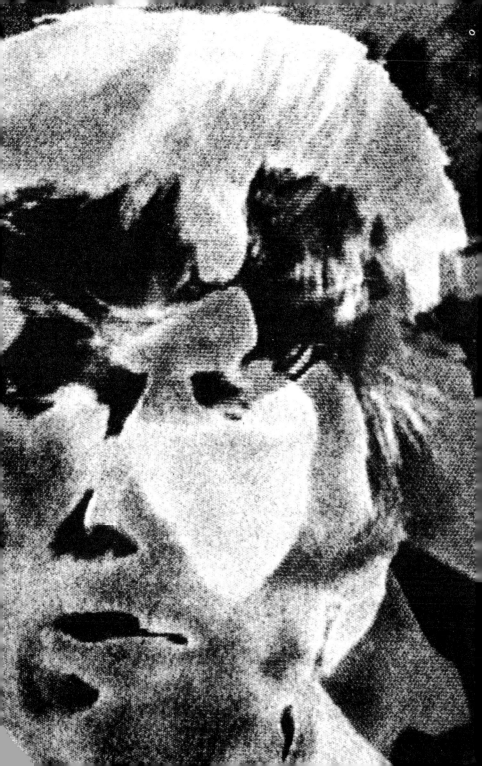

GIRL'S VOICE

In the beginning, God created the Earth, and he
said, "Let there be mud." And there was mud.
And God said, "Let Us make living creatures out
of mud, so the mud can see what We have done."
And God created every living creature that now
moveth, and one was man. Mud-as-man alone
could speak.

[STONY *bends over to pet cat*]

What is the purpose of all this?" man asked
politely.
"Everything must have a purpose?" asked God.
"Certainly," said man.

[*Cat walks away*]

"Then I leave it to you to think of one for all of
this," said God. And He went away.

[Scene changes to STONY *hitchhiking]*

[*Noise of vehicle approaching.* WANDA JUNE
appears on firetruck]

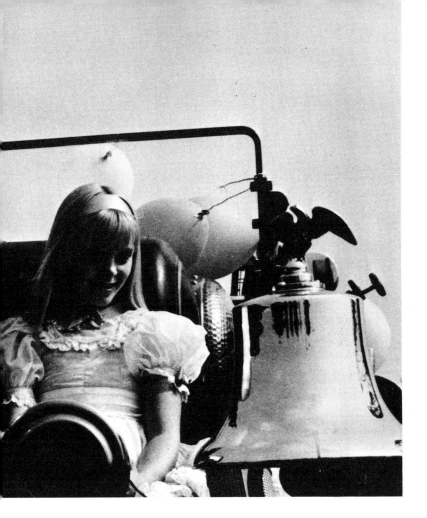

WANDA JUNE
Hi. Room for one more.

STONY
Am I dead?

WANDA JUNE
Nothing to be ashamed about. Hold on! Here we
go . . . !

251

WANDA JUNE

I am Wanda June. Today was going to be my birthday, but I was hit by an ice-cream truck before I could have my party. I am dead now. I am in Heaven. I am not mad at the ice-cream truck driver, even though he was drunk when he hit me. It didn't hurt much. It wasn't even as bad as the sting of a bumblebee. I am really happy here! It's so much fun. I am glad the driver was drunk. If he hadn't been, I might not have got to Heaven for years and years and years. I would have had to go to high school first, and then beauty college. I would have had to get married and have babies and everything. Everybody up here is happy—the animals and the dead soldiers and people who went to the electric chair and everything. They're all glad for whatever sent them here. Nobody is mad. We're all too busy playing shuffleboard. So if you think of killing somebody, don't worry about it. Just go ahead and do it. Whoever you do it to should kiss you for doing it. The soldiers up here just love the shrapnel and the tanks and the bayonets and the dumdums that let them play shuffleboard all the time—and drink beer.

[*Carnival music. Noises of happy crowd. The crowd moves into a large arena celebrating the arrival of* STONY.]

[The music comes to a discordant end as Hitler appears, goosestepping and snarling from the balcony.]

HITLER
What a poor specimen of a man you are.

STONY

That's been said before.

HITLER

Do you know who I am?

STONY

Yes. And you scare the hell out of me. I think
you scare me more than anything I've ever seen
in my life.

HITLER

I am death, and I am here to tell you all there is to
know about me.

STONY

[*Shaking his head uncertainly*]

I don't think so.

HITLER

[*Drawing himself up*]

You deny I am death?

STONY

I think you're my childhood dream of the most
terrible creature that could ever be.

[*Looking around*]

And I think that this is my childhood dream of
how God might try to make everybody happy
when they were dead.

HITLER
I am death, and I am final.

[*Aside, awed by himself*]

God, am I ever final.

[*To* STONY]

When I say the magic word to all these people,
they will vanish forever. I will then say the
magic words to you, and you, too, will vanish—
never to be seen again.

[*To the crowd, horrifyingly*]

There is no Heaven!
When you are dead, you are dead. That's all
there is to it.
There is no afterlife in any way . . .

[*One-third of the crowd vanishes*]

Shape!

[*Another one-third of the crowd vanishes*]

Or form!

[*Only* STONY *and* WANDA JUNE *are left*]

Go to the worms, you fool!

WANDA JUNE

[*Pitifully*]

The worms?

HITLER
To the worms, my blond, Teutonic child.

WANDA JUNE

[*Bleakly*]

Good-bye.

HITLER
Good-bye!
And then there was one.

STONY

[*Half to himself, a growing insight*]

Death in inner space.

HITLER

[*Sniffing insubordination*]

What's this?

[STONY *touches his head*]

STONY

It's all up here . . . you . . . them . . . this
. . . Mission Control . . . the moon, the sun,
the stars.

[*Growing stronger, a good man forced
unwillingly into a test of strength, supposing,
after all, that he might just win*]

I am going to make *you* disappear.

HITLER

[*Bluffing, hoping he isn't bluffing*]

How?

STONY

[*Bowing his head, patting it all over,
familiarizing himself with a powerful weapon
he has only now recognized as a weapon*]

Up there! I'll use this up here!

[*Raising his head, nearly ready for a test*]

There *is* an afterlife, if I create one up here.
I can create anything up here . . .

[*Meaning death,* HITLER]

or destroy it.

[STONY *and* HITLER *square off like wrestlers*]

HITLER

[*With mock lightness*]

Life against death?

STONY
Death against . . . imagination.

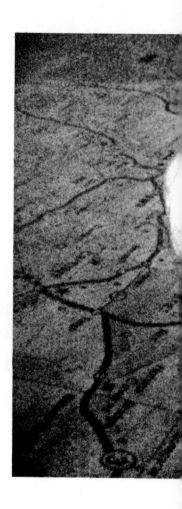

HITLER

[*Suddenly striking the first magical blow, not touching* STONY, *but closing his eyes and writhing with incredible body English, wishing him out of existence with all of his might.*]

Disappear! Disappear! Disappear!

[STONY *writhes, sinks to his knees, rises again, refuses at great cost to disappear.* HITLER *opens his eyes, sees that* STONY *has survived, becomes an old man of putty, such as* HITLER *became at the end of World War II.*]

So.

STONY

[With a gentle, sure gesture, quietly]

Disappear.

[HITLER *disappears*]

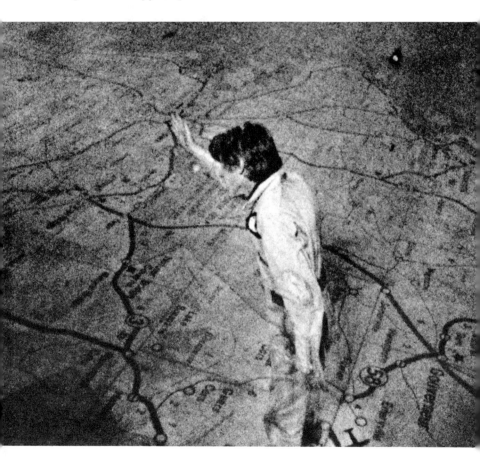

[STONY *alone, gestures*]

Appear!

[*Crowd appears in front of* STONY]

Disappear!

[STONY *alone*]

Appear!

[*Crowd appears*]

Disappear!

[STONY *alone*]

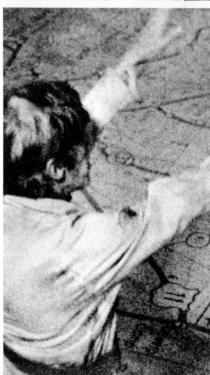

[STONY *working his way out of grave in Brooklyn cemetery*]

STONY

[*Reading epitaph on tombstone*]

"Stony Stevenson, Astronaut. Everything was
beautiful and nothing hurt." Oh, lucky me. Lucky
mud.

VOICE OF BOKONON
See what a nice job God has done.

STONY

[*Hearing* BOKONON'S *voice inwardly*]

Nice going, God. I certainly couldn't have done it.
I feel very unimportant compared to you.

VOICE OF BOKONON
The only way you can feel the least bit important
is to think of all the mud that didn't even get
to sit up and look around.

STONY

[*Standing up, wiping some of the earth from his space suit*]

I got so much, and most mud got so little.
"What's the use of worrying . . . it never was
worthwhile . . .
So pack up your troubles in an old kit bag and
smile, smile, smile"

[STONY *walks away from grave and approaches
a man with a lawn mower. Noise of lawn mower.
Noise stops*]

STONY

[*Pointing back at his own tomb*]

There's a tombstone back there . . .

CEMETERY GARDENER

A tombstone! An understatement is what that is.

STONY

It says, "Stony Stevenson, Astronaut."

CEMETERY GARDENER

He's not actually buried there, of course. That's just a memorial his mother put up. He's out in space or he's out in time. Who knows where he is?

STONY

Right. You know, it says on the stone . . .

CEMETERY GARDENER

"Everything was beautiful and nothing hurt?"

[STONY *nods*]

I thought everybody knew that.

STONY

I've been away.

CEMETERY GARDENER

His space capsule splashed down in the Pacific, right on target. But when they opened it up, it was empty. There was just a note in there, and a half-finished bottle of Tang. And the note said what's on the tombstone.

STONY

Thank you.

CEMETERY GARDENER

Any time.

[*He restarts his lawn mower.* STONY *walks
through the cemetery*]

"What the use of worrying? It never was
    worthwhile . . .
So pack up your troubles in an old kit bag,
And smile . . . smile . . . smile . . ."

Between TIME and TIMBUKTU

AN NET PLAYHOUSE SPECIAL

Produced by
DAVID LOXTON

Directed by
FRED BARZYK

Adapted for television by
FRED BARZYK
DAVID LOXTON
DAVID ODELL

Associate Producers
MATTHEW N. HERMAN
OLIVIA TAPPAN

Director of Photography
BOYD ESTUS

Sound
WIL MORTON

Editor
DICK BARTLETT

Casting
ARNOLD HOSKWITH

Costume Designer
PATTON CAMPBELL

Sets
FRANCIS MAHARD
CLINT HEITMAN

Assistant Costume Designer
PENELOPE BELKNAP

Choreography
WILMA CURLEY

Special Video Effects
DAVID ATWOOD

Gaffer
JOHN MACKNIGHT

Assistant Cameraman and Grip
ROGER HAYDOCK

Assistant Editor
STEVE SHANE

Stock Footage
DELL BYRNE

Graphics
EUGENE MACKELS

Additional Sound
DAVE LOERZEL

Music Consultant
JOHN Q. ADAMS

Production Manager
ELIZABETH O. DAVIS

Animated film designed by
RON FINDLAY
GAIL GUTRADT

Animated film produced by
Folio One Productions Ltd.

Supervision
AL BRODAX

Animator
MARTON OMMUNDSEN

Production Assistants
JANET OLIVER
TOM QUINN
PETE SCOON

Our thanks to Elkins Productions
International Corporation for
permission to include excerpts
from the novel *Cat's Cradle*

Our thanks to
Air & Space Gyro Services
Eastern Benson Gyro
The Holy Child Marching One Hundred
Massachusetts General Hospital
Massachusetts Metropolitan District Commission
Museum of Science, Boston
New York City Parks and Recreation Department
Paik-Abe Synthesiser
Queens Day Preparatory School
Quincy Market Cold Storage
Utility Supply Company
And lots of friends

Executive Producer
JAC VENZA